GW00498977

THE POCKET POWER BOOK OF PERFORMANCE

BYRD BAGGETT

RUTLEDGE HILL PRESS

Nashville, Tennessee

Published in Nashville, Tennessee, by Rutledge Hill Press, 211 Seventh Avenue North, Nashville, Tennessee 37219.

Distributed in Canada by H. B. Fenn & Company, Ltd., 34 Nixon Road, Bolton, Ontario L7E 1W2.

Distributed in Australia by Millennium Books, 33 Maddox Street, Alexandria NSW 2015.

Distributed in New Zealand by Tandem Press, 2 Rugby Road, Birkenhead, Auckland 10.

Distributed in the United Kingdom by Verulam Publishing, Ltd., 152a Park Street Lane, Park Street, St. Albans, Hertfordshire AL2 2AU.

Design by Gore Studios
Typography by D&T/Bailey, Nashville, Tennessee

Printed in the United States of America
ISBN: 1-55853-462-8

1 2 3 4 5 6 7 8 9 – 99 98 97

INTRODUCTION

When I wrote *The Book of Excellence*, I wasn't sure what to expect. All I had going for me were a hunch, some strong encouragement from friends and fellow professionals, and a few dozen powerful guidelines guidelines developed from nearly two decades of observing top performers in numerous fields: from conventional sales professionals to bankers, accountants, lawyers, doctors, stockbrokers, and others. These women and men had achieved their success by keeping it simple, developing positive habits, and being continually committed to total excellence.

What made *The Book of Excellence* so widely accepted was that the powerful guidelines I had developed found practical expression in the habits of these top performers. Different situations and different personalities resulted in different habits. Readers responded positively to the book's practicality. There were no radical new insights because there are no new secrets to peak performance—only the proven timeless principles by which successful people have always lived and of which we need to be reminded constantly.

My hope is that you might grasp these habits of peak performers and apply them to your own situation. Let these expressions of common sense be your guiding light to uncommon achievement. Best wishes in your personal pursuit of excellence.

Success at the expense
of faith and family
really is failure.

Proper planning
prevents poor
performance.
Remember this as
the Five P's.

EXCELLENCE IS NOT OPTIONAL.

Customers will find
a way to buy from you if
they like you. They will
also find a way not
to buy from you if they
don't like you.

Each day you get better
or worse. It's your choice.

Solicit feedback from your competitors' accounts. This is very useful for identifying ways to penetrate them.

∞

Don't put all your eggs (time) into one client's basket.

Plan your sales calls
a minimum of one
week in advance.

True wisdom is not a fad.

The customer's
perception is reality.

BE A TEAM PLAYER. PRIMA DONNAS DON'T LAST.

Always ask for the order!
Don't worry about the
technique or the style.

Have a single,
consolidated planning
calendar that you keep
with you at all times.

Be as critical of yourself as you are of others.

∞

Are you becoming complacent?

∞

Do you add value to your customer's business?

Develop a sense of
urgency to your work,
and pay attention to
the details.

You're not learning
anything when
you're talking.

What's your best remedy for when you are feeling down? Try making several new sales calls. You will be amazed at the results.

Don't be late for an appointment. (But it's all right for customers to be late.)

A BAD ATTITUDE
CANCELS ALL
OTHER POSITIVE
SKILLS.

Send birthday and
anniversary cards.

Push yourself. Only you
can motivate you.

Be a part of excellence,
not a critic of it.

Let your support staff
know how special and
important they are.
Be sincere when you
tell them!

Be open to change.

Spend a minimum of
four hours a day in front
of customers.

Breakfast appointments
create sales opportunities.
Clients tend to be fresh
and more receptive then.

Be yourself!
You can't fool the
audience.

Be a student of your
industry: trends,
competition, and niche
opportunities.

Great potential is one of
life's heaviest burdens.

Your time budget is as
important as your
financial budget.

Opportunities come in
unexpected packages.

Believe
IN YOURSELF,
YOUR COMPANY,
AND YOUR
PRODUCTS.

Keep your competitors on their toes!

The best defense is still a good offense.

Are your shoes polished?

Ask your customers to
audit your performance.
Their opinions are the only
ones that truly matter.

If you're not changing,
you're not in first place.

CUSTOMERS LOVE HUMILITY.

Be well manicured.

Follow the leader,
not the follower.

It is very important that
you like yourself.

A customer's opinion is
formed within the first five
minutes after you meet.

Look at life through the
windshield, not the
rearview mirror.

Set your watch ahead five minutes. You will be on time and will experience less stress.

Don't waste your energy on negative gossip.

Expect excellence from
yourself and others.

∞

Be serious about
your business.

∞

Get up early
and work late.

Have fun and celebrate
your successes.

Check the Help Wanted
section. This will help you
identify the most
progressive companies. They
are excellent sales leads.

Give business leads to
professional associates.
Most likely they will
return the favor.

Call someone you
haven't seen for a while.
Don't just think about
doing it.

Concentrate on sales,
not on marketing.

Be loyal to your employer.

Return calls within one
hour, if possible.

BREAK BREAD WITH YOUR CUSTOMERS.

Have a professional,
but not necessarily
expensive, wardrobe.

Monday mornings and
Friday afternoons should
be work time,
not wasted time.

Write it down.
Don't rely on
your memory.

Your time is important.
Expect others to make
appointments with you.

Resist fads, whether in
clothes or language.

∞

Develop relationships
with people at various
decision-making levels
within your accounts.
Personnel changes
are inevitable.

Underpromise, Overperform.

Ask questions and identify needs before you present solutions.

If you follow up, you will be a hero.

Knowledge without application is useless.

SEEK ADVICE FROM SUCCESSFUL PEOPLE.

There is a wealth of
opportunity for the true
sales professional in
today's economy.

Listen. Listen. Listen.

Dress conservatively.
This still conveys an
image of dependability
and responsibility.

Don't compete with
your customers.

Rapport is not developed
over the telephone.
Face-to-face interaction
develops long-term
business relationships.

Choose effectiveness
over efficiency.

Work harder and smarter.

Don't just go for the big hit. The greatest opportunities exist in small- to medium-sized companies.

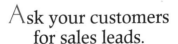

Ask your customers for sales leads.

The top 20 percent of
sales producers earn
sixteen times more
income than the bottom
80 percent.

Do it, don't just talk
about it!

Technology is not
a replacement for
hard work.

Rely on your support staff.
Your time should be spent
in front of the customer,
not in the office.

Always carry an adequate supply of business cards.

Spend two hours per week at home in creative thinking, planning, and working on sales appointments.

ALL PLAY AND NO WORK DOES NOT WORK.

If you were your own
competitor, how would
you win over your
accounts?

Know your market.
Where is the business?
Who has it?

Strive to make yourself
and your company
number one.

When you start taking
your customers for
granted, you start
losing them.

Emulate the habits of the winners, not the also-rans.

Be consistently persistent, but not a pest.

Don't slack up after a big sale. Turn it up another notch.

Motivation is what turns
knowledge and skill
into success.

Are you doing the same
things this year that you
did last year?
If so, you are losing
ground.

EXCELLENCE KNOWS NO TIME CLOCK.

Remember, it is harder to keep an account than it was to get it.

∞

Set goals. Monitor your status on a quarterly basis. Modify your actions accordingly.

Never say negative things about your company to your clients. Instead, communicate your concerns to your management.

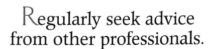

Regularly seek advice from other professionals.

Establish an exercise routine. This is important to your mental well-being.

You have a choice between developing good habits and developing bad habits.

Silence is a necessity,
not a negative.

Don't let your ego get
in the way.

Take an active role in
helping your community.

IF YOU ARE A VETERAN, LEARN FROM THE ROOKIES.

Send a plant to your
customer's open house.
This still works.

Watch the amount of
liquor or alcohol you
consume.
Your credibility could be
lost in one evening.

Use a beeper.
Thus the office can get in
touch with you when a
customer needs you in
an emergency.

∞

Observe and then
cultivate five habits of a
successful salesperson
you know.

TAKE TIME TO SHARPEN YOUR SAW.

Schedule daily quiet time for planning, relaxing, and brainstorming.

Carry an adequate supply of cash. Not all restaurants take credit cards, and it is embarrassing to ask your customer to pay.

Don't confuse efforts
with results.

Sell your customers what
they want, not what you
think they need.

Measure three times,
cut once.

Make two morning and
two afternoon
appointments your
minimum daily goal.

Do you thoroughly know
the features and benefits
of your products?

Check your breath before
you meet your customers.

Make sure your customers
know your product and
service capabilities.
It's amazing how many
do not.

Be nice to secretaries.

Do you create sales
opportunities or just
react to them?

Proofread all
correspondence.

Reserve a weekly
luncheon or dinner for
your spouse and children.
This is more important
to them than your
business successes.

Make appointments.
Remember, your client's
time is very important.

MOVE FAST.

Don't spend your time
worrying about why you
can't win an account.
Concentrate your thoughts
on how you will win it.

It's the small things you
do for your clients that
make you successful.

Participate in a
fellowship group.

Strive for increases in
profits, not just
sales volume.

Relationships require
more than one sales call.

Don't expect prime
accounts to be handed
to you.
Be proactive and develop
new business.

When you work hard,
you have earned the right
to play.

Do *what* you said you were going to do, *when* you said you were going to do it, and *how* you said you were going to do it.

∞

Spend as much time providing customer service as you do talking about it.

Know how your products
differ from those of your
competitors.

Invest your time
in learning,
not just in training.

Tell the truth!

Don't expect your customers to tell you they are unhappy with your level of service.

Pursue accounts that fit your profile for the optimum customer.

Don't dump all your products on your clients. Identify their primary needs and submit your solutions.

∞

Aim high. You normally hit what you aim for.

Make that extra call at
4:30 P.M.

Stop, listen, and think
before you respond.

Smile.
Customers like
positive people.

Read *Living Above the Level of Mediocrity* by Chuck Swindoll (Word).

Your chances for success increase in proportion to the number of sales calls you make.

Be concerned when you
lose, but never
feel defeated.

While out of the office,
call in for messages at
10:00 A.M., 2:00 P.M., and
4:00 P.M.

DON'T TELL YOUR CUSTOMERS HOW GOOD YOU ARE. SHOW THEM!

If you are not interested in the appetizers, will your customers invite you to share in the main course?

Invest your time in customers who have the financial ability to purchase your products or services.

Make a stop in the
bathroom before your
presentation. This is an
excellent time to check
your breath, teeth, and
hair, and check your
shoulders for dandruff.

Be nice.

ASK FOR HELP.

Don't handle
administrative duties
during prime selling time.

Be consistently aware of
how you are utilizing
your time.
Conduct monthly audits.

Take time to recharge
your batteries.
Rest is important.

Improve your speaking
skills by enrolling in Toast-
masters or by attending a
Dale Carnegie course.

Be a positive influence.
Others will emulate.

Congratulate your peers
on their accomplishments.

Thank your spouse for his
or her help and support.

PATIENCE IS A VIRTUE. DON'T GIVE UP!

Invite your customers out for a glass of iced tea or lemonade. You will be amazed at how much they enjoy the simple pleasures.

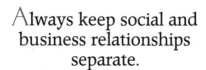

Always keep social and business relationships separate.

Never take your business
relationships for granted.

Believe in yourself.
If you don't, who will?

Be aggressive,
not oppressive!

If you smoke, don't light up in front of your customers.

Keep your car, especially the interior, clean at all times.

Success does not come easily. Are you willing to pay the price?

Carry your business card
file. You never know when
you will need a phone
number.

Remember that none
of us is more important
than the team.

NEVER ACCEPT MEDIOCRITY.

Be practical. Don't waste your time on conceptual training.

Learn from your mistakes, and take another approach.

Tenure without productivity is a liability.

Hold annual feedback sessions with your customers. You will be amazed at the benefits.

∞

"He who sows sparingly will also reap sparingly, and he who sows bountifully will also reap bountifully" (2 Corinthians 9:6).

If you can't find the time
to do it right the first time,
how do you find the time
to do it over and over?

Sales is like banking: You
have to make the deposits
before you can participate
in the withdrawals.

THERE IS NO REPLACEMENT FOR EFFORT.